Sri Ramakrishna

TELLS STORIES

Retold

SRI RAMAKRISHNA MATH

MYLAPORE, MADRAS 600 004. INDIA

Published by:
Adhyaksha, Sri Ramakrishna Math, #31, Ramakrishna Mutt Road, Mylapore, Chennai–4

First Edition, April 1982; Nineteenth Edition, First Print, March 2023
ISBN(13 digit): 978-81-7120-174-7; ISBN(10 digit): 81-7120-174-1
4000 copies
Printed in India at
Sri Ramakrishna Math Printing Press, Mylapore, Chennai–600004

God Resides in Everyone

It was a sunny morning. You know how cold it is in the Himalayas. In the very high Mount Kailas, it is colder still. So sunshine is most welcome there. It is a matter of joy. Lord Ganesh the darling child of Siva and Parvati, was feeling bored. He had none to play with. He thought he would run out into the garden and play in the sunshine.

He went to the kitchen. Mother Parvati was busy getting the food ready. Ganesh hugged her and said, 'Mother, may I go and play in the garden?'. 'All right, my boy,' said Parvati, 'but don't dirty yourself. And come back quickly, you have your lessons to do.'

Even before she had finished the sentence, Ganesh was gone. With a hop and a leap he was out in the garden. He plucked and smelt fragrant flowers. He chased the multicoloured butterflies. He climbed trees and ate the delicious fruits. He tried to catch the

deer, but they were too fast for him. All this running about tired him. He sat under a tree. Just then he heard a mewing. It was his pet cat greeting him. He looked at it fondly. It walked up to him gracefully and climbed into his lap. It closed its eyes and cosily settled down to a nap.

Ganesh felt this was not right. It is bad to sleep in the day-time. He should not permit it. He roused the cat. It opened its eyes a little and gave a small mew in protest. Ganesh stood it on its hind legs. He would literally teach it a lesson; stick in hand he asked pussy to repeat what he said. But the cat only blinked. It climbed back into his lap and closed its eyes again.

Ganesh was irritated. His pupil was getting disobedient. He caught hold of the pussy and scratched its face. The cat jumped out of his grasp and ran away. Ganesh smiled to himself. Cats will be cats. He roamed about in the garden for a little longer and then returned to the house.

He felt very hungry. He stepped into the kitchen. "Is food ready, mother?" he cried out. Parvati looked at him smiling and said, "Yes, Ganesh, go, wash and come. I shall finish dressing my wounds." Ganesh was puzzled. Wounds? He looked at his mother more closely. He got a shock. There were many ugly scratches on her lovely face. Ganesh became angry. "Mother, tell me who has done this to you? I shall tell Father and get the villain punished.'

Then he got a second shock. Parvati said, "The culprit is none else than my beloved son Ganesh". Ganesh could not make head or tail of what she was saying. "I hurt my dear mother! Impossible, even in a dream. And was I not all the while out in the garden? Perhaps some mischievous boy has taken my guise and done this wicked deed."

But Parvati only shook her head. "Ganesh, tell me, did you hurt anyone while playing in the garden?". "No, Mother," said Ganesh "I had no companion to play with today". "Then did you play with any pet animal and hurt it in any way?" asked the mother.

Ganesh now remembered how he had punished the disobedient cat. But what had that to do with the scratches on his mother's face? He questioned her.

Parvati smiled and said, 'Ganesh, don't you know I am the Mother of the whole Universe? It is I who live in all creatures. When therefore you hurt any creature you are hurting me."

Ganesh saw light. He now understood. He was only one of the children of the Divine Mother. She loves all her children equally and suffers equally with all. Bowing down before his mother, Ganesh told her "Mother, from today I will not hurt any person or any creature by thought or deed".

The promise Ganesh made, each of us has to make. Then only can we be really the children of the Divine.

Frog in the well

A frog lived in the village well. All its life it knew only the inside of this well. It had seen nothing of the outside world. All it saw were the pots the villagers lowered into the well to take water. So to the frog the well was the universe.

Once it started raining cats and dogs. The heavy downpour continued for a number of days. From somewhere another frog came and fell into the well. It had been living in the sea previously. Because of the rains it had escaped from the sea and sought the shelter of the well.

The frog in the well asked the new comer, "My dear fellow, where are you coming from? I don't think I have seen you before." The visitor replied, "I am from the sea. The heavy rains have made it very chilly out there. So I have come here. Can I be your guest till the rains stop?" "Oh yes", said the well-frog. "Remain in my well as long as you want. I have no good company to talk with. So you are quite welcome."

The well-frog took out some worms from its stock and offered them to the sea-frog for dinner. The two got on pleasantly.

After dinner the well-frog asked the sea-frog, "You spoke of the sea where you were living. What is the sea?" "O", replied the sea-frog," The sea is a huge mass of water." "Is the sea as wide as this?" The well-frog extended its two hind legs and pointed to the space between them. The sea-frog laughed. "The sea is much, much bigger than the space between your legs".

The well-frog looked at the sea-frog doubtfully. It extended its fore legs wide and asked "Is the sea so huge?" The sea-frog laughed all the more. "Far, far bigger," it replied. The well-frog's pride was hurt. It leapt from one side of the well to the other and asked, "Is your sea so big?" The sea-frog only said, "I cannot tell you how big the sea is. It cannot be compared with anything in this well."

The well-frog nearly burst with anger. "You are a liar," it told the visitor. "How can there be anything bigger than my well? Get out before I thrash you."

The sea-frog thought it wiser to jump out of the well. It returned to its limitless sea. It was convinced that it could not change the well-frog's ideas.

Most of us are frogs in the well. We have certain ideas and habits. These have come to us from the society in which we live. We think these are the only ideas and habits that are correct. We look with surpirse and hatred at ideas and habits that men in other societies have. We do not understand that our society is only a very small part of the world like the well. We must be broad-minded to tolerate and work with other ideas and habits, like the frog which understands the vast sea. To be narrow minded is to be a frog in the well. To be liberal-hearted is to be a frog of the sea. Now tell me, do you want to be a frog in the well or a frog of the sea?

How God was fed

In a village there was a lovely little Siva temple. A priest was regularly conducting the worship in the temple. He had a wife, a son and a daughter. The son was fondly called Sivakumar. The boy also was very much devoted to Lord Siva. He would often assist his father in getting things ready for the worship.

One day the priest had to go to a distant town to attend a marriage. His wife and daughter also were going with him. So he called Sivakumar and told him, "Kumar, mother, sister and I will be away for three days. I very much wish we could take you also with us. But the Lord's worship should not be interrupted. You have watched me and assisted me in the worship. Will you do the whole worship for the three days I shall be away?"

Sivakumar's eyes shone with pride and joy. "Father, you need not have any worries. I know all the details of the worship very well. I am blessed that I am given this opportunity to serve the Lord directly. All of you can attend the marriage carefree."

After the others had left at dawn, Sivakumar bathed, put on a silk dhoti and collected the flowers for the worship. He cooked the nivedyam carefully. After puja he placed all the dishes before the image. He drew the screen and waited outside for the Lord to finish his meal.

After twenty minutes he looked behind the screen. He was taken aback to see all the dishes as he had left them. The Lord had not taken even a particle of the food he had offered.

Sivakumar burst into tears. Addressing the Lord, he said, "Lord! why are you so harsh towards me? You accept the nivedyam offered by my father every day. But today you have refused to touch any of the dishes. Why this partiality? Have I comitted any mistake? Have I omitted to do any of the rites?"

The boy thought deeply for a while. He recollected every detail of the worship as done by his father. He too had attended to each of those details. He felt very much hurt. The tears from his eyes swelled to a flood. He could not see anything. He cried and cried.

This was too much for Lord Siva to see His child crying. Moved by the simplicity and earnestness of the boy, He came out of the image and ate all the offering.

The boy's eyes now glowed with happiness. The Lord had accepted his worship and his offering. He returned home in high spirits.

For three days the boy acted as the priest in the temple. All the three days the Lord accepted his worship and ate up all that he offered.

On the fourth day, the father returned home with his wife and daughter. Sivakumar was coming back from the temple after finishing the worship. Father embraced him and asked him, "Kumar, are you doing the Lord's service regularly?" "Very regularly, father," replied the boy. "Then give us the Lord's prasadam. We must take a little prasadam before taking our meal." But Sivakumar replied, "Father, no prasadam is left. The Lord has chosen to eat everything that I offered."

The father could not believe this. He said, "Son, what are you talking? Can the image eat the food placed before it? Do you not see that every day after the worship I bring home the prasadam? The Nivedyam offered to the Lord becomes prasadam. The Lord does not eat anything."

Sivakumar looked at his father in surprise. "Father, what you say is not true. God also must have food. When I offered the Naivedyam, He did eat it. What is strange about this?"

The father did not know how to convince his peculiar son. He said, "Kumar, let us see if what you say is correct. Tomorrow also you do the worship." The boy readily agreed. For one more day he could personally serve the Lord.

The next morning Sivakumar did the puja. He placed the dishes containing the nivedyam before the image, and drew the screen. He waited outside with his father, chanting the Lord's name. After half an hour the screen was removed. The father could not believe his eyes. Every dish was utterly clean. The Lord had indeed taken the boy's offering.

The father fell prostrate before the image and wept. He begged the Lord, "Give me the purity of heart that Sivakumar has"

The purer our heart is the nearer to us God is. When the heart is completely pure, God comes to us, talks to us and plays with us, just like any human being. The boy Naren, who later became Swami Vivekananda, asked Sri Ramakrishna, "Sir, have you seen God?" Sri Ramakrishna replied, "Yes, my boy, I have seen God and can show Him to you. Only you must weep for God."

By Rama's Will

Raghuram was a pious weaver. He was a devotee of Sri Rama. He firmly believed that everything happens by the will of Rama. The sun shines, the rain falls, the wind blows, men walk, fish swim--all by the will of Rama. If Rama's will is not there everything will come to a standstill. This was his strong faith.

Raghuram never forgot Rama. As soon as he got up early in the morning he would repeat the name of Rama. After bathing and offering Naivedyam to Rama, he would take his breakfast saying, "by the will of Rama". Again before starting weaving he would take the name of Rama. As he plied the shuttle, weaving the cloth, he would be chanting Rama's name.

He would take the woven clothes to the bazar for sale. If someone asked him what the price of a particular cloth was he would say, "By the will of Rama, the yarn costs Re. 1/-. By the will of Rama the labour costs 50 paise. By the will of Rama the profit is 25 paise. So the price of the cloth, by the will of Rama, is

Rs. 1.75p." Men and women would be charmed by his sincerity and simplicity. No one would bargain with him. They would pay him whatever he demanded. They were sure he would never overcharge them or cheat them. After the sales were over Raghuram would return home chanting Rama's name all the way. He would have his food and go to sleep again taking the Lord's name.

One night it was very sultry. Raghuram thought he would sit in the verandah for some time. He was chanting 'Ram, Ram'. A gang of robbers passed that way. They had burgled a rich man's house. They had a big bundle which contained lots of cash, jewels and other costly articles. They saw Raghuram sitting in the verandah. "Here is a hefty fellow. We can make him carry the heavy bundle", they said among themselves. They caught hold of the weaver. They put the bundle on his head and told him, "Walk with us, or else we shall thrash you". Raghuram, without any protest, went with them carrying the heavy load. He continued chanting 'Ram, Ram' all the way.

At the end of the street three policemen were doing their beat. The robbers got frightened. They ran away. Raghuram was left alone with the bundle on his head. He did not run away. He stood there chanting 'Ram, Ram'. The police opened the bundle and discovered the loot. They were happy thinking they had caught the robber red-handed. They marched Raghuram to the police station. He was kept in the lock-up that night.

Next morning the police produced Raghuram and the bundle before the Magistrate. They charged Raghuram with the robbery. The news quickly spread in the village. Men, women and children rushed to the court in wonder. Everyone knew what an honest and good man Raghuram was. How could he commit any robbery?

The Magistrate also had heard of Raghuram. He too could not associate robbery with this peaceful-looking weaver. But the police had caught him with the bundle. Anyway he thought, "I will not punish this man till I am sure he has committed the robbery. Let me ask him for his own explanation." He asked the prisoner, "Tell the court what exactly happened."

All the while, Raghuram was standing as if he was in another world. His lips were continuously moving, uttering 'Ram, Ram'. No

one who saw his face would think he was a criminal. Raghuram now turned to the Magistrate and told him in a clear voice, "Your Lordship, by Rama's will, I was sitting in my verandah. By Rama's will, some robbers came that way. By Rama's will, they put their bundle on my head and made me walk with them. By Rama's will, there were some policemen ahead. By Rama's will, the robbers ran away. By Rama's will the police arrested me, and kept me in the lock-up. By Rama's will, they have produced me before you. By Rama's will, you want to punish me."

Tears began to flow down the cheeks of the Magistrate. This man was so utterly like a child. He had nothing to hide. He was not calculating or clever in the usual sense. His trust in God was absolute. He must be not punished but worshipped

The Magistrate said in open court "I am convinced this man is innocent. I discharge him. Let him be set free."

Raghuram joined his palms before the Magistrate and told him, "BY Rama's will, you have set me free". The huge crowd assembled in the court shouted 'Jai Ram, Victory to Rama'. They took him in procession back to his home.

God Everywhere

A sage lived in a forest. He was as holy as he was learned. A number of bright young lads came to him to study. He looked after them like a father and taught them the greatest wisdom. Often he would tell them, "My boys! Remember, God resides everywhere and in every one. It is God that has become this world. You and I and all the beings we see are all God in different forms. Therefore never be unkind to any one. Insulting or harming any other is insulting and harming God himself. By doing wrong to someone you are doing wrong to yourself. So if you want to be happy, recognise God in everyone."

The boys were thrilled by this grand message. They went about their duties thinking of the meaning of what their teacher had told them.

Govinda was a very earnest student. He accepted every word of his teacher fully. He resolved that from now on he would look upon not only people but also animals, trees and stones as God. "What a grand idea this is! If every one and everything is God how can there be any quarrels or any sorrow? My salutations to the Guru. I will see only God everywhere. My bliss will be perfect."

One day the sage sent his students to the village to purchase the monthly provisions. Govinda was also one of the party. While they were returning along the highroad of the village, they heard a great commotion. People were running hither and thither. They heard someone shouting "The elephant is mad, run away from the road".

In fact a mad elephant was coming toward the students. It was trumpeting loudly in anger. It was the mahout or elephant-driver sitting on the back of the elephant who was shouting the warning. All the students of the sage except Govinda took shelter in the neighbouring houses. But Govinda stood on the road in the path of the elephant. "The teacher has told us that everything is God. The elephant also is God. I am also God. Why should God fear God?" Thinking thus Govinda did not move. The elephant driver shouted again, "Get out of the way. The elephant is mad." But Govinda stayed on.

The elephant saw the boy. It wound its trunk round the boy, and hurled him to the other end of the street. It then continued on its mad course.

Govinda lay on the road with a number of cuts on his body. His fellow students ran to the sage and told him all that had happened. The sage immediately came to where Govinda was lying. He had the boy carried to the hermitage, and nursed him well. In a couple of days Govinda was fairly well again.

The teacher now asked, "Govinda, why did you act like a fool? When the others ran away why did you also not run away?" "Master", said Govinda, "Did you not teach us that everything is God? Is not the elephant also God? What is there to fear from God?".

The teacher laughed and said, "You are a double fool. No doubt the elephant is God. But the mahout also is God. Did not the mahout-God ask you to get out of the way? Why did you not listen to the mahout-God? See the result."

Govinda now knew what seeing God in everything means. A spiritual person should not be a fool. We must not give up our common sense at any time. Seeing God everywhere means not being deceived by anything. We must see the reality and not be carried away by illusions. The inner reality is the same in everything. But there are differences in the outer forms. Wisdom lies in understanding the one reality behind the many appearances.

True devotion

All of you know about Narada. He is one of the greatest devotees of the Lord. Veena in hand he roams all the three worlds, singing the Lord's name. Every one respects him.

One day he came to Vaikuntha singing 'Narayana, Narayana'. Lord Vishnu greeted him and seated him comfortably. The Lord asked him, "Narada, you have been going round the earth. Did you notice anything special?" Narada drew himself up and said, "Lord! I do not know what to tell you. People everywhere are getting more and more worldly. They are getting absorbed more and more in the pleasures of the senses. Nobody has time to remember you. You must do something about it. Otherwise you will be completely forgotten. Your very position as the Lord of the Universe is in danger."

The Lord smiled. He can see readily what is behind the words and deeds of every one. He understood that Narada was speaking thus because he thought no one was so great a devotee as he. The Lord loved Narada dearly. So he wanted to remove the poisonous seed of pride from Narada's heart. He told him, "Narada, you go about singing my name non-stop. Hearing you, are not people inspired? Listening to you, will they also not chant my name?" This argument only increased Narada's ego. He said, "Lord! devotion is not easy. It is true I am spending all the twenty four hours singing your glories. But ordinary people cannot do like that."

The Lord was now sure that Narada must be taught a very good lesson. He said, "Narada, no doubt few can equal you in devotion. That is why I want you to go and meet the peasant Govinda in the village of Salagrama. May be, you may be able to know something more about devotion from him." Narada's pride was touched. Who was this Govinda whose devotion was greater than his? He must surely meet him.

Narada came down to the earth quickly. He located the village and spotted the residence of Govinda. This peasant was a poor man living in a hut. Narada watched his actions hiding behind a tree.

Govinda got up in the morning, washed his face and stood in front of the Lord's picture. He uttered Narayana, Narayana, Narayana, --thrice. He bowed down, then took his plough, put it on his shoulder and walked to his field. The whole day he ploughed and watered the field. At dusk he returned home. He took his bath and once more stood before the Lord's picture. He again uttered Narayana thrice. Then he took his food and slept. snoring loudly.

Narada was puzzled. How can this Govinda be a greater devotee than himself? Perhaps the Lord was pulling his leg. Straightway he returned to Vaikuntha.

"Narada, did you meet Govinda?" asked the Lord with a smile. "Yes," replied Narada, "I found your Govinda. But you could have told me you were joking. This Govinda utters your name only twice a day. He is completely absorbed in his field. I sing your name all the twenty four hours. And you compare Govinda with me!"

The Lord continued to smile. "Narada, could you do one thing? Please bring a cup filled to the brim with oil." Narada brought the oil-filled cup. "Now go round this assembly thrice with the cup in your hand. But see that not one drop of oil is spilt." Narada did as ordered. Holding the cup very carefully, he completed three rounds. Not a drop of oil was spilt. With a proud smile he said to the Lord, "I have passed your test. But tell me why you wanted me to do this."

The Lord asked him, "Narada, while making the rounds, how many times did you utter my name?"

Narada was upset. He said, "Lord, what a question to ask? You wanted me to see that not a drop of oil fell down. Attending to that, how can I utter your name?"

The Lord burst into laughter. "My son, you could not get time to utter my name even once while attending to the cup of oil for a few minutes. Look at Govinda. He is running a family with all its cares, but he manages to utter my name before he starts his work and again after finishing the work. This means while doing his worldly duties, he is always thinking of me."

Narada's pride in his devotion was broken. It is not the number of times that the Lord's name is uttered that matters. It is constantly remembering him under all conditions that is true devotion. Whatever you do, remember him.

Seek Wisely

Gupta was a merchant. He used to go from place to place canvassing business. He travelled widely and amassed much wealth. He loved pleasure and led a comfortable life.

Once he had to pass through a wilderness. There were very few houses on the way for miles and miles. He had started early in the morning. By noon he had walked a lot and was utterly tired. The sun was blazing hot. Fortunately he came to a big tree. It had many spreading branches. Under its shade he felt cool. He sat down exhausted.

"Oh how hot it is! If only I could have a cup of water. The thirst tortures me." As soon as he said this a lovely cup full of sparkling water appeared near his hand. In great wonder Gupta took the cup and drank the water. He felt immensely relieved.

What he did not know was that this was not an ordinary tree. It was a Kalpavriksha, the heavenly wish-fulfilling tree. Whatever wish a person expressed under the tree would be fulfilled. Not knowing this Gupta said, again to himself "My thirst is gone, but not my hunger. If only I can have a good dinner!" The next moment Gupta could not believe his eyes. Before him there lay a number of plates. On them were beautifully arranged various items. There was rice and curry, milk and sweets and many other delightful edibles. Eagerly, Gupta tasted one dish after another. Everything was delicious. The hungry merchant ate his fill. His hunger was more than satisfied.

The long walk in the heat, followed by the heavy meal made Gupta drowsy. He murmured to himself "I feel so sleepy, but how to sleep on this rough ground? It is full of stones and thorns. If only I had a thick soft bed!" At once a luxurious bed was beside him. Gupta stretched himself on the bed. He felt extremely happy. It was as if he was in fairy land. Whatever he wished was coming true. He wondered what this tree could be. "How is it that anything I say under this tree becomes real immediately? But then, can I go to sleep in this wilderness? There is no one within miles to keep me safe company. I am alone. Suppose a tiger comes this way!"

Before the words were out of his mouth, a fierce tiger sprang upon him from nowhere. It gave Gupta a mighty blow and in a few moments tore him to pieces and ate him up. That was the end of all his wishes.

God is a wish-fulfilling tree. Whatever we pray for sincerely He gives. So we have to be careful about what we pray for. We must beg Him only for lofty things like wisdom and devotion. If we ask for petty things of the world, He will give them to us. But then these things finally lead to trouble and misery. We shall be courting unending unhappiness. The best prayer, however, is to ask for nothing in particular. Leave it to God to give you what is best for you. He knows far better than we. So what he gives of his own accord will always be far superior to what we can even think of. Let Him give us as He wills.

Knowledge that Saves

Rama Sastry was a great pandit. He knew many Sastras by-heart. He could argue brilliantly and quote profusely from memory. In any debate he always won. The simple villagers would wonder how so small a head could contain so much knowledge. And Rama Sastry's pride was as huge as his knowledge.

One day he wanted to attend a debate to be held in a town on the other side of the river. The winner in that debate would get a big reward. The pandit came to the river ghat. He hailed a boatman and haggled with him for a long time. Finally, the boatman agreed to ferry him across the river for 25 paise.

The pandit got into the boat. He was the only passenger in it. So to spend the time he started conversing with the boatman. He boasted about the number of Sastrashe had learnt. He mentioned the different scholars he had defeated in debates. The pandit said, "My dear boatman, the purpose of human life is to learn as many Sastras as possible. What Sastras have you studied?" The boatman humbly said that he was illiterate. But everyday he prayed to God. The pandit said it would not do. Had he not studied the Vedas? The boatman said he had not even heard the name. The pandit declared, "You have wasted a quarter of your life. I myself have taken ten years to master the Vedas. All right. Tell me, have you read at least the Bhagavád Gita?" The boatman hung his head and said, "Master, I know nothing about the Gita." The pandit smiled scornfully and said, "Then half your life has been wasted."

After a few minutes the pandit asked him again, "You have read the Ramayana and the Mahabharata, I suppose?". The boatman remained silent. The pandit said "I can only pity you. You have wasted three-fourths of your life. Try to learn something in the quarter of your life left." The boatman looked sad.

As they were talking, a storm began to blow. The boat started to rock violently. It looked that the boat would topple and sink. The boatman addressed the pandit with joint palms. "Venerable sir, I am afraid we have to abandon the boat. I hope you know swimming, Sir."

The pandit was taken aback. "No, no, I had no time to learn swimming. I cannot float on the water even for a few minutes. Please save me." The boatman replied, "I cannot save you, only the knowledge of swimming can save you. It is true that I do not know

any of the holy texts. I have wasted three-fourths of my life. But I know swimming, and that will save my life. What a pity you have not learnt swimming. You have wasted the whole of your life." With these parting words the illiterate boatman swam to safety. The learned pandit found the bottom of the river.

Knowledge is not for show but for use. It should make you humble and not proud.

Stop not till the goal is reached

Somiah and Rajiah were neighbouring peasants. Each had two acres of cultivable land, side by side. But the two men differed in their nature. Somiah was hard-working while Rajiah was lazy. Once there was failure of the monsoon for two consecutive years. The drought was terrible and the land lay parched. Starvation faced the peasant families. Somiah was a man of action. He told himself; "Somehow or other I must get water to irrigate my land. My canal is dry but there may be some river beyond from where I can fill my canal". He went searching. God favoured his industry. He came upon a river in which there was a good flow. Somiah started cutting a canal from the river to his lands.

He had left home early in the morning. At mid-day he was still busy with the spade. The sun overhead was scorching. Somiah was perspiring profusely. But he was not aware of the sun or the sweat. Nor did he remember that he had not eaten anything since morning.

At noon Somiah's wife sent her daughter to call her husband. The girl said, "Daddy, it is noon. You are late for your bath and lunch. Mother says come home, eat and then come back to work if necessary". Somiah smiled at the little one and said, "Meena, I must finish cutting this canal. Then only I will have joy in eating my food. Go home. I will come later. Don't disturb me." The girl returned home and told her mother what father had said.

The clock showed three. Still Somiah had not come. His wife became anxious. She herself went to the field. She told her husband, "Why are you delaying like this? The meal has become cold. You always go to extremes. Come away with me. You can do the rest of the work after taking food." Somiah saw red. In a harsh tone he told her, "What a foolish woman you are! Don't you see, for want of water the crops are drying. All of us will be starved to death. I must first bring the water into the field this very day. Nothing else matters before that." His wife trembled to see her usually gentle husband so furious. She beat a hasty retreat.

Somiah went on digging till it was eleven at night. The river was now connected to Somiah's field. Water started gurgling into the land. Somiah's heart also gurgled with joy.

Somiah returned home. From the gate itself he called out, "Kamala, bring me oil for my bath." He had a comfortable bath. Then he sat down before the leaf lovingly spread by Kamala. He ate remarking again and again, "Oh, you are a wonderful cook! Your dishes are so delightful!" He ate to his fill, chewed pan, lay down on the mat and started snoring loud.

When Rajiah heard that Somiah was digging a canal from the river he too went to the river and started digging. At noon his wife also came to him and asked him to go home with her for food. Rajiah agreed, "Well, as you are calling I must come." With the spade on his shoulder he returned home. He ate sumptuously and slept well. In the afternoon he did not feel like returning to the river. The next day also he had other work to attend to. The canal digging got postponed again and again. During the critical days the crops did not get the needed water. They dried up completely.

In a few days Somiah's land was a laughing green. The paddy plants bent down with heavy grains. Rajiah's land on the other hand was a desolation.

Somiah worked on and on till the goal was reached. Rajiah stopped in the middle, and the goal escaped him. Whatever we undertake we must complete before resting. Our motto should be 'Thorough'.

The Lion that Discovered Itself

Gopala was a shepherd boy. He had a fine flock of sheep. Everyday he would take the sheep to the forest. While the sheep grazed on the green grass and leaves, Gopala would climb a tree on the river bank and play on his flute.

One day Gopala saw from the top of the tree a lioness lying dead on the river bank. Beside it lay its lovely newborn cub. Gopala came down from the tree. He understood what had happened. The lioness had jumped across the river from the other bank. She had been big with child. The effort made her deliver the cub. But the effort also took away her life. So the cub was an orphan. It looked very pretty. Gopala took the cub home. He gave it sheep's milk. He kept the cub in the shed along with the sheep. He gave the cub grass and milk. So the cub grew up amidst the sheep. It went with the other sheep to the forest. It ate grass and drank sheep's milk. It bleated like a sheep. Thus in every way it grew up a sheep.

One day a big lion sprang upon Gopala's sheep grazing on the river bank. Gopala had gone away a little distance on some other business. The terrified sheep ran off in all directions bleating. The lion cub also followed the running sheep bleating. The attacking lion was surprised. It could not understand why a lion cub was afraid of lions and was bleating like a sheep. It pounced upon the lion cub and held it between its paws. It told the cub, "What a fool you are! You are not a sheep. Look at me. You are a lion just like me. Why do you bleat and eat grass?"

But the lion cub did not believe the lion's words. It was sure it was only a sheep. So it continued to bleat. The lion however would not let it go. It took the cub by its neck to the river bank. The lion said, "Look at your image in the water. Do you not see that you and I look alike?" The lion cub, in great fear, looked at the two images in the water. It was surprised to find that its own image was exactly like that of the lion, only on a smaller scale. It looked at the lion in surprise.

The lion now gave a loud roar and said "You also roar like me." The lion cub at first only bleated. But when it tried again it found its real voice. Presently it was roaring like a lion. It began to enjoy the roaring. After a few trials it roared in chorus with the big lion.

The lion wanted to complete the education of the lion cub. It killed a deer grazing near by. It thrust a piece of the deer flesh into the mouth of the lion cub. The young fellow had been eating only grass till now. But the flesh, freshly killed, was tasty. So it ate the flesh with delight. Then it gave a tremendous lion's roar without any prompting from the lion. Finally the lion and the lion cub walked away into the depths of the forest.

We are all like the lion cub which had forgotten its real nature. Everyone of us is a spark from the divine fire. But, we do not realize this truth. It is only when a great soul tells us and proves to us our real nature that we give up our weaknesses and become divine. We must not be sheep. We must grow every day more and more into our lion nature.

The Blind Children and the Elephant

In a town there was a school for blind children. Teaching blind children is difficult. They are unable to see things. So they do not have any proper idea about most things. They have to use their imagination to understand things.

Once, the teacher was telling them a story about an elephant. The children asked, "Sir, what is an elephant?" The teacher said, "I cannot describe to you what an elephant is. But I shall take you to an elephant. You can touch it and understand what it is." The children were all happy. They could by personal touch know what an elephant is.

The teacher took the children to the Manager of a circus nearby. He told the Manager, "Sir, these children are all blind. They want to know what an elephant is. Can you please permit them to touch a real elephant?" The Manager looked at the blind children. He was moved with pity. He called one of his assistants. He told him, "Take these children to our elephant.

The assistant led the teacher and the students to a tree to which the elephant Radha was tied. He asked the elephant-keeper to allow the children to touch the elephant safely. So each student was permitted to touch the elephant. All of them surrounded the animal. One of the boys moved his hand over the large ear of the elephant. He caressed the ear with his hand and thought to himself, "The elephant is like a fan." Another boy held a leg of the elephant with both his hands. He decided, "The elephant is a big pillar." A third one touched the trunk of the elephant. He understood that the elephant is like a thick club. Another touched the stomach of the elephant. He concluded the animal is a huge jar. Everyone was delighted. All of them returned with their teacher to the circus Manager to thank him.

The Manager asked them. "So all of you have touched the elephant. Tell me, what is the animal like?" Each boy began to say what he felt. The first blind boy said, "Sir, the elephant is a huge fan." But the second boy interrupted, "No, no, you have not understood properly. The elephant is a big pillar like the one we have in the school verandah."

The third boy laughed and said, "What fools you are! The elephant is neither a fan, nor a pillar. It is a big club as we have in our gymnasium." The fourth boy now intervened. He told the Manager, "Sir, none of these has felt the elephant properly. I will tell you what it is. It is like a huge jar. Is it not so, Sir?"

The discussion became warm. The students began to quarrel among themselves. The Manager smiled and asked them to stop the discussion. "I will tell you what the elephant is. Each one of you is right and all of you are wrong. Each of you has touched only one part of the elephant. From that knowledge you have tried to describe the whole elephant. This is not correct. The elephant is like a fan, like a pillar, like a club and like a jar. But it is something much more than all these. Only if you see the elephant as a whole can you know what it is. So don't quarrel with one another."

We are all like these blind children when we quarrel about the nature of God. Each of us can know only a small part of the infinite God. We must not limit God to what we have experienced of Him. God is the sum total of the different experiences of different men and much more than that. We have to be humble when talking of God. We must admit that other views about God can also be true.

The False Turns True

In a village there was a fisherman. He loved comfort. He would tell himself "What is the point in working so hard? Let others work hard to make money. I can steal their money and lead a happy life." Thinking thus, he left off fish catching. All day he would sleep or gossip with friends. In the darkness of the night he would enter the house of one rich man or another and steal whatever he could manage.

One night he entered the garden of a big Zamindar. In it there was a big pond reputed for its huge fish. The fisherman's greed was roused. He tossed his net into the pond and started dragging it to haul up the fish. In the process he could not avoid making some noise. The Zamindar's servants heard the noise. They lit a torch and began searching the whole compound to find the cause of the noise.

The fisherman was in a fix. Presently the servants would discover him. "Oh! they will beat me black and blue. How can I escape? Lord, please save me this time. I promise I will not thieve again." Somehow the prayer soothed his nerves. He got greater confidence. His brain became clearer. In a flash he threw away the net. Nearby there was a heap of ashes. The gardeners had, the previous day, burnt there the fallen dry leaves. "Ah! This is fine. Let me smear myself completely with the ashes. Then these men will not be able to recognise me." He threw away all his clothes except a kaupinam. He liberally applied the white ashes all over his body. He closed his eyes and sat in padmasana.

So when the servants came to the pond, they found an ash-smeared man. "Oh! A great sadhu has come here to bless us. He is doing meditation at a lonely spot in the darkness of the night. Our master is a very pious man. He will certainly be happy to know this." The servants ran to their master and said 'Lord, a holy man has come to our garden. He is absorbed in deep meditation on the bank of the pond.' The master at once came to the pond. He fell flat on the ground in prostration before the ash-smeared stranger. "Maharaj, I am blessed that such a holy man like you have chosen my poor garden for your tapas. If you had intimated me earlier I would have provided a more comfortable location for your meditation. Anyway please remain here as long as you wish. Myself and all my people are at your service to do whatever you need."

The fisherman who had been trembling with fear till now, felt a sudden change. "I was fearing severe punishment but here I am being invited by the Zamindar to stay on comfortably. It is only the grace of the Lord whose name I have been taking the last few minutes as a pretext. Lord, I promise you I shall give up thieving completely if I can get out of this place unharmed."

The next morning the news spread that a holy man was doing penance in the Zamindar's garden. Men and women, boys and girls began to pour into the garden to have the darshan of a great Yogi. The fisherman continued to sit with closed eyes. The devotees brought him fruits and flowers, gold and silver. By noon the spot where the fisherman sat was like the shrine of a temple. Hymns were chanted and songs were sung. Periodically lights were waved before the ash-smeared fisherman. It was only late at night that the crowd dispersed, promising to turn up again the next day.

"What a miracle!" thought the fisherman. "I have only been pretending to be a holy man. For that I am being honoured so much. If I really turn into a holy man who can say what all honours will not come my way? But then today's experience has taught me a great lesson. Holiness is its own reward. After resolving to lead a holy life, how petty of me to think of the rewards I can get! There is only one reward worth working for and that is devotion to the Lord. May He give me unflickering faith in his Lotus Feet! Attaining His love I shall have nothing more to attain."

The next morning when the villagers came to the Zamindar's garden to have darshan again of the holy man, they found his seat empty. He had gone away in the darkness to do real meditation far from the madding crowd.

Even a pretended piety can transform a life and make it blessed.